About Christine Swanberg

This is the newest book by a phenomenal poet.

Although most of the sonnets in this collection were written very recently, other newer free verse poems and poems from past publications have been incorporated to expand the collection in a more dynamic way.

Christine could be described as a bohemian who has a toe in Emily Post's Etiquette; an intense Scorpio hidden by a Libra ascendant and moon in Gemini jumping in the 9th House; a person who lives several lives simultaneously; a spontaneous free spirit with a penchant for perseverance. Her hub is the Midwest, but much of her life has happened bi-coastally, internationally, and in favorite haunts.

As a young English teacher, one of her first published poems was "Sonnet for Live Words," which appeared in ENGLISH JOURNAL nearly thirty years ago. It became a promotional postcard for The National Council of Teachers of English. The poem was written as a creative writing class assignment along with her students.

After decades of free verse, hundreds of poems published in many journals, as well as several collections from various presses, she returned to the sonnet for a challenge and a change. She wanted to see where the sonnet form might lead - and discovered the freedom the sonnet gives to keep it short and concise, ending with a little epiphany couplet. She found the Year of Sonnets a challenging and rewarding palette cleanser and is ready to return to free verse with renewed vigor.

WILD FRUITION: SONNETS, SPELLS, AND OTHER INCANTATIONS

New and Selected Poems
by Christine Swanberg

The Puddin'head Press
2017

Cover photo by Jeff Swanberg
Interior photos by Jeff Swanberg

First Edition
2017

ISBN#978-0-9819756-3-4

Dedication

To Joseph and Ann Rinaldi,
in gratitude for their unending generosity

and

Frank Schier,
who started it all.

To Jayne—
with best
wishes
Christine Swanberg

TABLE OF CONTENTS

I – YOUR GREAT ADVENTURE

II – A DARK THREAD

III – WINTER SPELL

IV – ASK THE GARDENER

V – WILD FRUITION

I—YOUR GREAT ADVENTURE

On days when you think there is nothing
to be thankful for,
begin with the faucet you tweak
to the perfect temperature,
the shower cascading,
massaging your neck and spine.
Consider the soft water you rely on
that allows lather to rise on your head,
or the stout hands of the invisible dishwasher
that scrubbed your pots while you slept.
Notice the curtains that frame the window
to whatever day will be discovered,
aroma of good coffee brewing
in the timed coffee maker
about to rev up your engine,
dollop of cream
from Oreo cows munching grass,
the toaster, the toast,
and marmalade,
grain, crunch, and fruit.
Reach for bifocals on the end table.
Pet the dog or cat who says good morning
with its nose or tail or nudge.
If there is someone to kiss,
know you are blessed.
Open the front door as you do each day
for the paper delivered by the paper boy
on his pre-dawn rounds.
Listen to a sparrow,
then the radio humming and talking,
song or voice that buoys you
in just the first hour of this day.

Something So New

I want something so new
a red door opening to a bright empty room
filled with sun
a window framing a stunning new vista
shimmering with adventure
perhaps a sea with its waves
that roar with promise
or a mountain across a still bay
glimmering with snow
as fresh as new beginnings

I want something so new
a bright empty room to stock
with vintage pillows and a sofa
for huddling and cuddling
the old cat who will have to learn
a new routine too
new places to stroll
new faces to explore
the possibility of unexpected friends
like a slew of gliding pelicans

I want something so new
that it sweeps me away
electrifies each sense
the possibility of being thrilled
or challenged like a heron
finding fish in a new pond
the lure of music yet unsung
dances not yet danced
the baggage left behind
the chance of reinvention

Driving north in Iowa, the Great River Road
   before us, the March thaw sprinkling sunlight
on blue icy patches of river, we pass bridges
   and dams where eagles spend the winter fishing.
Their huge nests rest in tree tops that line
   the river's edge. Silver glints of river carp in beaks
catch the sun's wink as the eagles carry on.

When you think of resolution, how your life
will fledge and wing despite its threat of extinction,
   or conflicts reaped upon the unsuspecting earth,
think about the eagles who survived,
   their perseverance even in ill-advised slaughter,
how they rose against the odds, catch fish
   as seasons turn. Think of the Mississippi River,

its pilgrims and refugees on barges and boats,
   the current that leads on to a distant place,
the promise of new life. Driving closer to Dubuque,
   we watch the hills grow jagged, pass
towns with names like Luxemburg,
   sheep peaceful on rocky hills, that first
spring green promise now sprigging forth.

Bridges

My first memory of them is the Lincoln Bridge
that glides over the Illinois River in LaSalle-Peru,

a stretch between the coal mines of Spring Valley

and the green leafy canopies of elms
of the rich Northern city, where my father

escaped to find a better life. Forgive me—

I have always been thankful for this choice
not to live amongst the tree-laden shanties

of coal towns, mean old men, and small minds.

I too have no wish to return.
The bridge and its wide expanse of water

remain the only beauty I carry from that bleak place.

Yet I still seek bridges away from my Northern city.
Bridges stretch like hope,

transitions to the place you must go to save yourself.

When you are in some sad space,
think about the bridges you have already known.

In the Ticino, small stone Roman bridges arch

over blue pools of mountain waters that rush
each spring when snow gushes from peaks.

In summer languid bathers stretch on rocks

beneath such bridges, the air so fresh and clean
it frees the breath.

The Bridge of Lions crests over the Matanzas River

in St. Augustine, where dolphins dance
near boats with black sails.

Invoke the bridges you have known

when you seem stuck on a confounding shore.
Recall them: small bridges on winding roads

where only one car can pass at a time, or

magnificent bridges like the ones you find
in great cities. Call upon the one that stands

foremost above your mind's swirling rivers.

Ask that bridge for the answer you seek.
Feel it carry you on its sleek, steel spine.

Know that no matter how tense and turbulent

the waters spin, you want to keep living in a world
where bridges keep their promises:

They take you to the place you need to go.

Convertible Mind On The High Road To Taos

Some mojo lurks in mesa shadows:
unexpected darkness in the Sangre de Cristos,
parched day, top down and burning,

hanging around a mountaintop cemetery
in a state that allows people to bury their dead
on their own land with a wooden cross,

where handmade motorcycles grace a new grave,
jazzy angles like Chimayo weavings
disturbing clouds-- low hanging baskets

changing with each new crest of wind.
Spanish missionaries must have had fierce thirst
dehydrated enough to hallucinate

such bloody icons at the Santuario de Chimayo—
stench of paraffin, decay, incense, rotting pine
nightmare of healing mementos clasped on chain link fence—

so many crutches, such faith. Do you want to believe
it's not a hoax? Do you want to believe
in childlike faith that works miracles?

The High Road to Taos asks questions
you thought you already answered.
Feel the Native presence breath and beat—

wisps of pinion, purple sage, whipping Apache winds
rattling dust and rocks,
your sense of reason lifting out of you

like a clay bowl emptying
where science loses its grip
your mind now open as the scalding sky.

The circle reigns in the kivas
near the threshold of the Taos Pueblo
where sunbaked women fish round loaves
or roll the dough into perfect globes
press the center in as though
they'd form clay bowls.

It fills the iron pot
and puffs up like a patty pan squash.
Their earthen urns have loaf-size rims,
centers pearled and leather-thin,
and etched into their sides—
the angled stamps of ancestors.

They weave their baskets
spinning a pot of reeds.
And here the smoke forever twines
around the terra cotta walls, where
the Sangre de Cristo mountains
wrap around them like a shawl.

Black Mesa Magic

Purple streaks in her hair, feline face,
slinky body, the wine mistress chats
about the tortoise-shell cat
who looks just like the one

I am missing, a thousand miles away:
weird Halloween black and orange cat,
more like a capuchin monkey,
goofy humanesque face. I'm enchanted.

She says, "New Mexico
is the oldest wine making state.
Missionaries had to have their wine."
The red Zinfandel is left-field delectable:

deep earth bouquet,
color like the Sangre de Cristos
at certain sunsets, a finish like velvet incense.
O happy camper palette. I wonder

if long- stemmed glasses
are the modern trailer park cousins of chalices,
kindle the thought of everyday sacred,
the sipping of wine its own ritual,

here at the Black Mesa Winery,
across the road from the Rio Grande.
I take my treasure to the gazebo
already grateful for the pleasure

of this moment, desert rose and sage
adrift in the wind, then a hurricane of hummingbirds—
Lilliputian acrobats darting, tumbling,
and twirling, a private Cirque du Soleil.

Now the wine master himself arrives.
"Black-chinned hummingbird," he says
when I point to one I don't recognize.
"Ah," I say. "Ah." We all sip red.

Don't tell me happiness is an illusion
when a trinity of favorite pleasures—
cats, wine, and hummingbirds—
converge on this sunniest of days

in the Sangre de Cristo Mountains,
the Rio Grande, the waterway that leads
the hummingbirds to this tiny santuario,
a thousand miles from home again.

Santa Fe Logic

Sure, the Santa Fe Square bustled
with rich old hippies and gypsy jazz,
a sliced melon moon and Venus hung low
like a dangling earring
in the black Southwestern sky.
Sure, the vegetarian meal at Case de Sena
sparkled, a garden of twinkling lights
that matched the stars,
the gift of handmade lapis earrings,
small sunflower tiles
and gratitude for a place in America
that hasn't been turned into a mall
or gentrified beyond repair.
Truly dazzling was not having to pay
Hotel Fonda parking even though the car
occupied space all day and into the night,
even though I ran into the hotel lobby
to pay the parking fee, astonished to be told,
"There's no charge if you leave after hours."
"Let me get this straight," I said. "You're saying
that if we had left at 5 pm instead of 10 pm
we would owe $20, but because we left at 10,
it's free?" "Yep," the bell hop answered."
"Cool," I said, and pocketed the bill.

Pear Blossoms

Rain on attic dormers,
Debussy,
and pear blossoms bursting

outside the window
like the string of fireworks
exploding during Chinese New Year.

In the Lahaina twilight,
mixture of sulfur, sea salt
and plumeria.

Rain quiet on the roof,
open window,
cardinal calling

and pear blossoms breeching
like the whales on Kaanapali Bay
that perfect February day

in the year of the Golden Dragon,
in the year of our Lord, 2000,
post-millennium madness.

Potion of Kona coffee,
squeeze of lime on the lanai,
folds of Molokai's mountains.

April bellows through attic windows,
thunder, and the pear blossoms
I've waited for all year unfurl

this vast and sacred year,
solitude my deliberate companion,
and private rituals open like pear blossoms.

What Sedona Says: A Sonnet Triptych

A rainbow slivers over Cathedral Rock
here, in Sedona, where molecules spin,
buzz up your spine, tingle your scalp, and knock
at the portal of your third eye. Within
each breath you take upon this vortex,
the meditations amidst red towers
cleanse and sharpen your cerebral cortex.
Then you might decide to pass the hours
communing with the great benevolence.
And if the ghost of Edward Abbey flies
as a vulture, or if you have the sense
that a restless spirit from Jerome cries
in the lightning of an afternoon monsoon,
breathe in, be one with each sacred ruin:

With each sacred ruin and cave dwelling,
with each red spiral and divine design,
with each hovering rock and cloud swelling,
with every desolate abandoned mine,
with every crystal, misguided or not,
with every hummingbird and mountain quail,
with the rattlesnake tied neatly in a knot
behind the cactus, and the wind's wail
over spires, through never ending canyons,
along green rivers winding, and sage brush
rippling by its side, sweet smell of pinyons
high upon the great red rocks, the green, lush
surprise near the rim of clouds, then the sun
like a thousand painted ponies on the run.

Like a thousand painted ponies, sunset
thundered through the ever changing sky.
The wind, rocks, spirits and the rain all met
that night just beneath the moon's cat eye.
Here is what the wind said: Keep moving.
The great red rocks shouted: There's always more.
And the dime store psychic said: Keep grooving.
And the rain whispered: Don't close the store.
They call to the secret shaman that lives
within your heart, the one who remembers
the soul of every living thing, who gives
the earth its sacred space, who numbers
herself among the little lizard, desert doves,
among every creature that she loves.

At The Sacred Cliffs Of Kauai

No matter how wide nor deep
today's grief, remember:
the world is wider and deeper.
When you feel it shrinking, know:
new earth still forms,
volcanic fire on the sea.
There may come a time when
things won't get better,
but not today
with its cleansing rain,
its hope of rainbows,
its change of plans.
Even the planets retrograde
and don't fall from their orbits.
In a million years, the Na Pali cliffs
will be nothing but a coral reef,
but see how they do nothing
to speed their erosion. Be like that.
Stand hard in your grief,
and let elements pound your ribs,
carve out something solid,
a jagged beauty unsurpassed,
pierced and pointing to the sacred.

Paradigm Shift In The Pacific Northwest

In the Victorian Era rich people taxied boats
to great arched rocks just to shoot puffins
from their nests. Even the women aimed rifles
at the flaming orange, gross beaks,
hard to miss, dropping the birds
into slashing waves that swooshed and whirled
the dashed bodies out to sea. For pleasure. Sport.

Today we tilt toward Orcas whales,
hoping for a breach or spy-hop, eager
for the brilliant black and white crests,
the bold dorsal fins in sync, circling, circling
like the great gears of a grandfather clock.
We lean nearly overboard, armed with binoculars
for but a blink of calf with mother.

We stand in honor of killer whales, our secret
collective wish that one will break the law of distance
imposed off the coast of Discovery Island, here
in the San Juan de Fuca Straits, where we funny folks
in hats and hoods hope a curious killer whale forgives us.
Come closer. Come closer. Our collective prayer:
Don't leave us now. We'll make amends. Come closer.

At Three Arch Cape

Oceanside, Oregon. 7 a.m.

Low tide and empty beach.
Even the mist incandesces below
Three Arches, their peaks like primitive gods.

A faint rainbow forms
around them perfectly
like a shrine.

Last week's measured life
with its compromises
like broken sand dollars vanishes.

On the great redwood's limb
now bleached bone-gray:
our initials, JS/ CS.

Who could guess a couple
married for forty years?
Still, today I walk alone,

head down my favorite inlet,
past the familiar shanties
and new condos rising:

misguided fortresses
that trespass shifting dunes.
No matter what—I still return,

and when I round the bend to Netarts Bay,
the entire village, old and new,
is fodder for the fog pierced only by pelicans.

High hum of wind and gull's shriek.
Today this beach with its shells
and parables is my companion,

and you, drinking coffee,
reading newspapers, you're earthbound.
I'm all tides and fog.

Only give me these dreamy mornings to keep.
Let me sit again on burnt driftwood, my back
against a dune, sing again the song

that ends in Sanctus, Sanctus.
It is enough to count myself among
the lucky, plucking perfect agates

and Holy Ghost money from sand.
And you in your blue stocking cap
and black leather jacket, waving.

Your Great Adventure

In every great adventure a dark thread
winds, serpentine. Were it not so, wisdom's
hard-earned skin, rough diamonds, could not be shed
along the rocky path that leads to freedom's
shining shore. In every great adventure
some black seeds are sown amidst the green.
Were it not so, only mediocre
smooth paths, manufactured jewels, would be seen
here in this ever-changing universe.
A little risk and danger spice the pot.
Compassion comes from many wounds to nurse.
If you're lucky, you'll draw the winning slot.
Welcome contrast, sun and rain, summer, snow.
This is what all great adventurers know.

II—A DARK THREAD

Cosmic Stew Complaint Sonnet

There are those who would tell you how to live,
no matter what their own track records are,
no matter how little they have to give,
no matter how transparent the scar.
They act like they know each passing guru,
up close and personal, the best of friends,
have all the answers to this cosmic stew.
But if they hurt you, don't expect amends.
They're above it all, detached, more evolved,
enlightened, self-actualized, and awake.
If you should have a problem unresolved,
they'll just say, "Let them eat celestial cake."
They cling to every new and passing trend,
and still don't know what's real and what's pretend.

A Few Ways To Look At Rage

Rage opens the door to a room
　that needs to be cleaned,
de-cluttered, re-arranged, and re-painted.

Rage is the bonfire of dispossession,
　like prairie burning
to set the soil free to grow again.

Rage is the crate of repossession,
　the taking back, the ultimatum you keep
when detritus and decay delay and defer.

Rage is the red-hot alert, the call to action,
　the gift of change, the straightened spine.
When the virtue of patience falls flat on its face,

consider its fiery sister, Rage. Consider Pele,
　goddess of the volcano. See how she makes
new earth form from lava, steam and water.

Fear's the fierce tiger
with claws curled,
but courage
is not the whip unfurled,
nor the cage.
A quiet voice tames rage.
Faith is a wing
or oiled lock,
a wild iris growing
from forever rock.
A cage with rusty lock
is comforting
to anyone with broken wing,
but broken wings will mend
and from caged doors ascend
a winged tiger.

A Few Ways To Look At Deception

Deception grows like a volunteer sapling
unwanted in a sunny garden, perhaps the heart.

If left untended its roots burrow deep into the soil,
down into the labyrinth of veins and promises.

Soon it's taken hold, digging trenches, like an army
on the frontline, starving out the enemy and the conscience.

Deception collides like a cold and hot air mass
swirling over cornfields, gathering speed, a vortex

of destruction, galloping horseman of the apocalypse.
If longs to tear your roof off, leave you devastated in debris.

It's the tornado of your worst swirling nightmare,
and it wants your little dog too. Make no mistake

when deception comes dancing like Calypso. Say:
No thanks. I've had enough for a lifetime. Goodbye.

If it comes in a pretty bottle, read the contents: Arsenic.
Sure to kill by slow degrees. Or faster if preferred.

For the record, deception's not the white lie you tell
an aging friend fishing for compliments on a bad day.

It's the domino factor.
Remember King David and Bathsheba?

One big lie: good men dead, accomplices scattered like
garbage.

Deception takes prisoners, my friend. Think twice about
the email from an old flame that betrayed once.

Stay clear from anyone who smiles
while using you like a plastic card of infinite credit.

Know this: Deception has no boundaries. Like murky
clouds covering the eclipse of the shadowed sun,

it blinds you before you know it.

One October Morning Past Your Prime

There may come a moment
face to face with destiny
the flash of insight
that if everything stayed
exactly as it is
you would be complete:
the futile wish to keep
from changing.
Call it gratitude
or call it melancholy,
the lightning knowing
things are as good
as they are going to get.

Does the flicker circling
the locusts last golden leaves
this October morning
feel the same
within its wings and bones?
Will the solitary dove
overstay again this year?
Will the old demented fox
running sideways to catch a squirrel
finally come no more
to the russet prairie grasses
graceful in their temporary dying?

Somewhere in the sinews
of our used monolith of muscles
we who have moved
past our prime know
we are the lucky ones
to come this far
and live so well
amongst the trees and grasses,
leaf fall and chilly breeze.

Suppose one day long past your prime, you made
a poor judgment regarding laundry, mixed
vintage tablecloths in hot water, paid
the price with all the backgrounds blue-jinxed.
Suppose you pulled each precious piece to find
them all a little blue: beige to baby blue,
red to lavender. Then the day defined
itself in blue: email stuck in cyber glue,
the phone call that jarred your mood, the invoice
incorrectly calculated, a friend's
unexpected lecture, the needling choice
to respond or not when something dear ends.
On those days when blue prevails from the start,
there's not much you can do but guard your heart.

Blue-Jinxed 2

Guard your heart against seeping indigo
that bleeds into the cauldron of the day:
the sneaky comment, the swirling mojo,
the unmet gaze, the multi-tasking way
we ignore each other to distraction.
Perhaps some baby blue string pulls you
into melancholy's dark attraction,
mellow as the blue bird's ironic hue.
You are not somewhere over the rainbow
and you doubt that any pot of gold waits
for you—and the only time is now.
Now—all sorts of blue pushing at the gates.
Some days are a long laundry list of blue,
scalding mistakes, no getting over you.

One November Morning Past Your Prime

You come to see
  you are not part
of any tribe or clan,
  walking a trapezoid,
not a circle or square.

Lone wolf, butterfly,
  solitary cloud, secret shaman,
keen resister of all Groupthink.
  You are not lonely:
Solitude is a rich uncle.

You kept the sacred promises
  you made in distant years,
in that deep, reclusive silence,
  that stillness that propels you,
shrewd star that streams through shadows.

About Time

Perhaps some wisdom resides in your limitations.

If you want to be authentic, be careful
not to trade one tribe for another.

Cancer isn't caused by bad thoughts.

Don't confuse love with pity or you might
spend your life with the wrong people.

The number of calls you receive on your cell phone
is not the measure of your importance.

Technology is a tool, not a destination.

Jealousy serves no purpose: note the lousy in it.

If you don't cultivate solitude or court silence as a friend,
you may find yourself lonely in a room full of noise.

If you haven't seen the stars in a while,
it's about time.

She keeps a fake snakeskin box
in the black lacquer night stand
that sits by the sleep number bed
she adjusts to perfection each night.
Yet sleep does not come for long.

She wakes at the witching hour,
flips the switch, opens a book but never
the diamond-backed box filled
with discarded people
that scour her dreams.

No forgiveness, only denial
delineates the logical creases
of her perfect brain.

    Blame
      is her game.

Crammed into the box are all
who do not fit the perfect puzzle
of her latest desire. One by one
she eliminates those who hold her dear
no matter how her world shrinks
with each abandonment.

The discarded do not speak
but at the witching hour wiggle out,
wrangle and rattle. They're the conscience
that lies dormant during day, the blame
that sways like a little black stone
in her heart, the skin
she won't shed in the light
but wriggles off in the black night.

Dangerous Woman

The cosmetologist with the white streak
like a skunk's in her black, big hair, meant no harm.
How could she know "amber champagne"
would turn the old lady's hair pink,
the same shade as my first Barbie doll's?
Or that just a dab too much alcohol
in the cotton ball used to swab
a brow line could trickle and burn,
turning the eyelid red and swollen for weeks?
Once a year an eyebrow goes missing.
Well, there are pencils for that.
Is it possible that she didn't hear
when asked to go easy on the mousse,
gel, and spray by the woman who always
goes straight home to wash the gunk out?

What was she thinking
when she married someone named Benjy?
The canine name should have been a clue,
not to mention his black motorcycle,
not quite a Harley, and his drug use—
just some pot, coke, maybe a little meth,
and an ex whose name spells Trouble
or his two-year-old, already on Ritalin.

Yes, she's a dangerous woman
though she never meant any harm.
She reads the Tarot, sings karaoke off-key,
has a pit bull named Baby.
She lives with her cousin, Vinny,
until things settle down,
which they never do. Which is why
she runs late, keeps clients waiting.

Every night she eats out,
knows every new chain in town,
orders every Kevorkian special.
If it's deep fried, her name is on it.
She makes my mouth drool
with descriptions of jumbo margaritas
and cheesy appetizers.
And what a buffet of dating services,
set ups, blind dates, and parties--
a dazzling new hair style or color for each.
A new pair of skin-tight jeans,
lacy camisole with cleavage,
really high heels or jet-black boots,
new shade of acrylic nails, glitter.
Once, she woke to find a man dead in her bed.

Do I want to strut my stuff all over town?
Give up choir for karaoke, or
the good husband
for a string of hot dates that don't lead anywhere?
Sensible shoes for stilettos?
All I know is this: She never meant to do any harm,
but she's a dangerous woman,
a woman with chemicals, Marlboros,
and a lighter that works. Watch out.

Texting Terrorist

My thumbs, my thumbs, they ache,
thumping the steering wheel,
the cold steering wheel, the cold
impotent steering wheel. My thumbs
long to tap, tap, like an acupuncturist.
I need to look down, I can't help it:
Everything is urgent,
can't wait, can't trust. Anxiety
in my thumbs, my eyes, my throat.
I need the little shining box.
It lets me know everything's OK.
I gotta go for it, gotta put that little
Ark of the Technological Covenant
right on the steering wheel.
Right there. Gotta know if anyone
likes me. You understand. Someone
does: Dude, wtcha doin? B thr n 5.
The little god sits on my lap now,
a little vibration, nice, man.
My personal lap of luxury,
my pal, more loyal than a dog
and a lot less work.
Gotta look down. Gotta see
this little light of mine, gotta let
it shine in the car, the cold car,
on my lap, thumbs going like
knitting needles, so urgent,
I am all thumbs, thumping thumbs.
Omg omg omg.
Missed the stop sign, man, omg.
Swerved on ice, omg. Crashed
into red SUV with kids, dog's
barking from car.
Can't remember what to do.
Text my friend. Says call 911.
Cn I txt 911?

When the last train trembles
    silent in its tracks
and the telephone's ring becomes
    its whistle
or a lone gull's cry
        go
where you can be smaller
    than a hummingbird's egg,
or where you can dance
    anonymous in purple socks.

Wear a cape with stars sewn on,
    a periwinkle ascot
and unbecoming bifocals. In fact,
    unbecome altogether.
        Unbecome
the brown and black jackets
    hung straight
these working years. Unbecome
    your dreams of pencils,
black coffee, tests already passed.

Let loose
    the leather leash of approval.
Bark at anyone
    who insists you heel.
        Bite
the hand that feeds you.

Backroads, 1982

I
You like to be alone.
You camp,
watch moths burn
in wonder.
I see your brown corduroys,
your boots, leatherlaced,
your knees up.
You are contemplating
something I do not see.
I am driving my fast car
on these backroads
and know we would be friends.
I like to be alone,
but I am still turned
too inward.
I have not become
the moth, the fire,
the dirt in my nails.
But slowly, slowly,
I am becoming
this thin road,
this fog,
these sparse Midwest trees,
the squirrel and the crow.

II
A shooting star pierces
a field of wheat.
There is a crater
in my hand.
I want to turn toward you.
In our open palms
stars locked,
and I cannot unlock them.

The best I can do
is the worst I can do.
Accelerate.
Turn up the radio.
Drive home again.

III
Tonight, on this late road
when the sky is past indigo
and the stars are just there,
I light a cigarette
and blast the radio.
Van Halen screams:
Jump. Go ahead and jump.
My foot arches
against the pedal.
One hand grips the wheel.
I race the yellow line
and think of you again:
having to get somewhere
but not knowing where:
something like going home:
something about being lost
in a galaxy
that might be lost
in a universe.
I like to think
I know where I am going.
How hard for you
unable to say
who you are
or even pretend.

Embrace Uncertainty

When uncertainty hangs humid
Thick as a steel-gray sky
And you can't tell if a storm hovers
In the charcoal clouds
Or if only a gentle Zen rain will follow,
Return to that still, quiet place.
Imagine you are the water itself,
The deep center of a blue, glacial lake,
The sizzling tide pulled back to its source.
Know that whatever rain must come
Has its purpose if you wish to find it.
The rain takes many forms, gathering
Its legions with the wind, which might be
Sweet spring breezes or wind sheer
Pulling pines and locusts from their roots.
Embrace uncertainty as a cloud holding water,
Building its cumulous castles in the stratosphere,
Until release comes, and come it will.

It wasn't that there were so many friends
or that my life there had been so perfect.
It's just that how you look at it depends
on whose scheme of things you hold in suspect.
What was it to me that men were lovers
or that a goat or two were glorified?
I never cared how others passed their hours.
I kept a good house and was occupied
in covenanted duties. It was a life.
It was all I knew. And what would you do
if someone said, "Don't look back"? Like a knife
the words hit their mark. Mind bleeding, I knew
my fate: I had to be the one to look
and turn to salt--a lesson in their book.

Cheating Grief

Should you find yourself un-sprung
by grief, like cranking gears
of the old grandfather clock
that you must rewind
forward each half hour,

know: You can't cheat grief.
If so, you'd skip a chime,
which might end up as an extra heartbeat.
Yours. Plus—you'd have to start again.

Once I tried to cheat grief
claiming to detach from it,
jetting off to the Big Sky
leaving grief at home on my pillow.

When I looked up at the Seurat sky,
I felt the dead I cherished, wept mercilessly
under the Milky Way, each shooting star—
someone I would never see again.

Shadows, dark and sweet,
  a place of retreat—
but you don't have to stay
  no matter how cozy,
nor wake to the slug tugging
  at your heart.
Where is it written
  that you don't deserve
to shine when even scientists admit
  we come from star dust?
You don't have to be the sun,
  moon, nor meteor—
only the little flame
  that sputters and glows.

III—WINTER SPELL

If each ornament is a memory,
mixed blessings hanging from your tree,
handle them gently, wrapping them
in soft tissue rolled into the box
you will place in the dark basement corner.

In the dark basement corner of your mind
you can box the harder memories
for another year. They are safe
and so are you this day of new beginnings.
Another year has lent its logs to the fire.

Another year has lent its time to you.
So unwind the little lights and lay them
down like large nests, empty for the winter.
Uncoil the snares and scars the year has wrought.
Conjure all the good from the year's cornucopia.

From last year's cornucopia, conjure the good.
Rewind the victories, the delicate surprises,
those things you did not expect but received
amidst the hard-earned bricks and mortar.
Remember what will buoy you this new year.

This new year, remember what buoys you
through the tumult and chaos that surrounds us.
Remember kindness, the uncle who loved you best.
Recall the ruby amidst the costume jewelry.
Wear it like a talisman throughout the shining new year.

January Spell

Magenta sunset points like a pine tree
from the corner of my bedroom window.
All is quiet here this January.
The cat snuggles against my pillow.
Dusk brings colors magnified by winter
when stars begin to hang like ice sickles.
The indigo night begins to enter
and softly from its corners tickles
Venus and Saturn near the ringed moon.
Come, O winter night to bless our slumber.
From your vast horizon—a silent tune.
May our dreams be light and unencumbered.
Rise and cast your spell, cold winter night.
Under blankets of deep sleep, dreams take flight.

One January Morning Past Your Prime

Minus six degrees, frozen ribbon of dusky red
behind the trees, this sunrise.
Sun on windowpane terrarium—
ferns, sparkling diamond seas,
Lalique birds floating over crystal mountains.
Wrapped, warm in your white robe,
coffee with cream, engine starting slowly,
but starting, starting. This day
when most stress and striving leave footprints
behind you heading to the finish line,
more like a turtle than a hare.
Marvel at destiny, good fortune,
despite the Sherpa's pack of obstacles
on your back. You stood the course,
perseverance, a life coach shouting
behind the scenes. How you kept your promises
to arrive here,
this cold morning past your prime,
in your warm house, free from mortgage
or wayward desire that fueled
the person you used to be
before you saw the world,
before your loves, your scars,
your betrayals and compromises,
the hard won victories,
windfalls that flew in like wayward swans,
myriad kindnesses like flocks of sparrows.
The casino still jingles,
your bets are hedged toward more,
a bird or two in your pocket.
Marvel at the cardinal that endures sub-zero,
bright red and full of fervor,
waiting to take flight one more time.

The Butterfly Tree
--for Karla Anderstatter

Like monarchs returning to the Butterfly Tree,
large snowflakes sale past the window,
landing on the overgrown junipers.
Snow butterflies landing like sunshine.
I know a woman who lives where
a real butterfly tree grows sideways from a hill
near the San Andreas Fault, nearly wind-thrown.
Deep-rooted, it survives Pacific gusts, floods,
and even the earth swaying beneath its fingers
doesn't send it crashing. There each November
monarchs would return, awaited like a lover's call.
In those days, they returned in droves
thick as snow. Orange boughs.
And when many died, as butterflies do,
she took them in
and scattered them on her Christmas tree.
At this moment, it's January in Illinois.
A pair of cardinals search for juniper berries.
Delicate talons leave a soft snow calligraphy.

February Morning

This bitter cold February morning
somewhere twixt solitary and lonely
so quiet you hear your mind exploring
dark familiar paths. You think if only
this, if only that, then what might have been
in your parallel universe, the place
all your daring dreams dance. Remember Zen,
all unfolding process, eager white space.
Remember nothing but what's before you
this winter day filled with promises:
savor lunch with a friend, chai tea to brew,
a car that starts, a cat to feed, dances
to salsa in the den, suds and shower.
You move ahead, ready for this hour.

The Long Winter Procrastinates

The long winter procrastinates this year
like a difficult decision. To stay
or leave? The voice is not so crystal clear.
Is it a groove or rut we must obey
when all our senses stick like ice dams clogged
with winter inertia within our veins?
O, if only our minds could be de-fogged.
O, if only we could release the chains
that bind us to a life lived under par.
See how the crocus finally fights through soil
hard and cold? Such icy courage goes far
and yet comes so naturally without toil.
Perhaps the answer lies in staying still,
flowing with the force, let come what will.

When the world is a black and white photo
and all the trees are defined like bare bones,
and the snow-ladened pine makes a grotto,
and winter whipping wind whimpers and moans,
then we rest inside our hearths unencumbered.
We kindle the fire, turn inward desire
to things long forgotten, now remembered.
And if we might ask what this day might require,
the answer may be sublime or serene:
a closet or book, a movie or nook,
a project put off, some silver to clean,
perhaps something quite delicious to cook.
You must find something so good to savor
if you want to stay in winter's favor.

Snow Salsa

Dancing with the wind, slanted snow swivels,
salsa slashing the windows. We're snowed in.
A corner ice sickle hangs and drivels
like an intravenous glucose machine.
I put on "Tropicales" and dance too,
a solo sequestered salsa (of sorts),
a solitary rendezvous, not blue.
Midwesterners must always be good sports
when winter comes conquering and calling.
We dance and read, watch old movies, maybe
paint a closet or polish brass. Befalling
all it can befall, snow on limb of tree.
Stay and salsa a day, you swaying snow.
Just a day, OK? Then you have to go.

Place seven stalks of day lilies
   in a vase hand-painted with swans
during the hour of the crescent moon in Gemini
   when Venus ascends at twilight
and Mercury retrogrades in the Ninth House.

Turn off all clocks and appliances.
   Drape lace over the television.
Lay the vase upon it. Light five red candles
   that have the fragrance of cinnamon
in a circle on the kitchen table. Remember

one Christmas from a past life
   in another country or a dream
where Chagall donkeys danced on roofs
   and lovers floated unencumbered
under Capricorn. Stir together cardamom

and nutmeg. Sprinkle over the candles
   while singing a torch song.
If every flame remains, five wishes will
   come true. If even one goes out,
there is something you must do. Do it.

Then wave a wand of crystal sugar.
   Invoke the saints of childhood
even those who blessed you with the gift
   of pain. Especially those. Twirl
a ruby ring around your index finger.

Use a black swan's feather and yellow
   parchment. Hang the parchment
over the bathroom mirror, and no evil
   will live there or anywhere in
your house where only the enchanted live.

Winter Spell

When Venus glides by Mars, and seven planets
   stitch a diamond necklace
under Capricorn in the southwest twilight,
   and a tangerine moon rises
like a Phoenix through murky clouds, find

a Depression Glass vase. Imagine
   the midwife who kept in near her canary
long before you were born. Listen to them.
   Recite all the blessings of the year,
even those you didn't wish for. Especially those.

Place orange Bittersweet and a few Chinese lanterns
   in the vase, invoking lost loves
that have brought you to this cold enchantment.
   Lay the vase on a window sill where
the moon cast long shadows through the trees

and a cat with one good eyes might sleep
   curled in a grapevine basket
next to The Dreamer's Dictionary from Good Will.
   Find the last five dreams you can
remember, reading their meanings softly.

Arrange them into a story that begins with
   Once upon a time in the Land of...
and ends with Lived happily ever after.
   Tell the story to someone you long for.
Then, looking out the window, remember

footprints in hard-packed snow: cat, deer,
   rabbit, raccoon, crow, sparrow.
Remember them as you brew hot tea:
   mint, chamomile, and rosehips
in a Nippon teapot from Salvation Army.

As the tea steeps, find a ring of moon stone,
   opal, or coral and read woolen scarf.
Wearing them, mix a potion of pepper, nutmeg and curry in a wooden bowl.
Sprinkle in the doorway and sneeze thrice.

Sing a song from childhood. Any song
   will do. Return to the tea, adding
cream and honey before you drink it slowly.
   When steam fogs the window, no evil
shall enter where only the enchanted live.

Lines Written For Charlotte In Bronte Country

"I see at intervals a cage; a vivid, restless captive is there;
were but free, it would sour cloud-high."   Jane Eyre

No forest breaks the bony wind settling
like a skeleton in the moors and heaths
of Yorkshire. Winter creeps into small bones
where brownstones creak like old mastiffs.
Cuttle-boned, sharpened in this loving cage,
you stayed within the Haworth parsonage
until you woke like a hummingbird and flew
above the heather on the greening moors.
The yarrow is fragrant on these rocky crannies.
Yet the landscape broods. Shadows covering
the fields like ghosts, hovering.

Before Grooming The Horse In Winter

Mare searches for old kernels with her nose
and finds them lodged within the burry spears.
She wants the bundled bales but she's not close
enough behind the bales to reach the tiers.
A loose whinny drops her liquid muzzle,
and when Bruce the brown tomcat wraps his tail
around her fetlock, their noses nuzzle.
She rolls him. He leaps to the highest bale.
Her icy tail whips against an old gray
plank, sets Bruce upon his haunches, but she
forgets their game, content to munch away.
They touch like willow blossoms in the barn
and speak a language I'm too fast to learn.

Accidental Trumpville

Searching for eagles on the Great River Road, Iowa side,
quaint stretch of highway that leads to Lock #12
on the Mississippi River,
where January eagles congregate and fish at the dam.
High in a bare tree, a lone young eagle perches.
But at Lock #12, no eagles.
At the Richman Diner, we ask the whereabouts of eagles.
No one knows. One theory is that it isn't cold enough:
When the Mississippi doesn't freeze,
eagles can catch food anywhere.
They are used to the eagles and don't seem to miss them.
The waitress is kind and splits our order happily:
homemade chicken and dumpling soup and club sandwich.
These are the folks who were left behind.
Behind the counter, Fox News is on with no sound.
Heading back, we see a garage with antlers,
a sign that says John Wayne Drive. Since the last time
we searched for eagles here, businesses have closed.
I can't tell if it's the sky alone that's gray and hazy
or a miasma rising this murky Monday
after the inauguration. Sad for so many reasons
and no eagles to give us hope.

She waits for you like a long-lost lover
whose earthy fragrance she cannot forget.
Musty, moistness she wants to uncover,
the dopamine burst, the shattered regret,
the winter-starved soul in great need of sun,
muscles releasing, the bone-thawing rush,
crocus erupting, tight bud's explosion,
fresh sea of grass, breathing, chartreuse lush
greening, new bird's preening, all around song.
Come thrush and thrasher, cat bird and blue jay,
ruby-throated hummingbird. It's here you belong
every year without fail. So stay
with thunder in your pastel palette, spring.
You're welcome here no matter what you bring.

IV—ASK THE GARDENER

Hummingbird Whisperer

Glory be to the fierce little warriors
who return to my garden each year.
Come, enjoy, drink the various nectars,
tiny bold ones. You without any fear.
Teach me to cultivate fervor and focus.
Stay in our shared secret sanctuary
created for you with bergamot and phlox,
fuchsia and the feeder hung on the tree
you visit each morning. Hello! Goodbye!
Who could be freer? Fast as a torpedo
when I'm digging, spading, you catch my eye.
Faster than the wind glanced from my window.
You share delight with your earthbound sister.
You've made me a hummingbird whisperer.

Ask The Gardener: A Sonnet Triptych

If you want to know how the earth changes,
each year bearing one more scarring,
scalding the soil's surface, then rearranges
the system beneath the soil, marring—
ask the gardener on her knees. She will tell
you how she's watched and witnessed
day by day, year by year, the darkened spell
of careless winds and tainted rains, the flood
and parching bi-polar seasons, distressed.
She will tell you how sorrow's in her blood
watching all the life she considers blessed:
today a lone monarch lands on milkweed,
where once a dozen hatched and danced, then sailed,
where once the creatures that she loved prevailed.

If you want to know how the earth is tipping
with each up-close-and-personal invasion,
ask the gardener with her bucket, dipping,
filled with black beetles not in the equation
that balances the garden: creatures devouring
the native plants provided for safe keeping
of the bees, butterflies, and birds; scouring
each buckthorn, rose, and milkweed—feeding
frenzies, insatiable, in black swarms.
Ask the gardener when the bees disappear
before her eyes, or when dry earth warms
and turns from black to gray, a cracked mirror.
Where once the gardener laughed with easy sighs,
now the gardener stoops too full of goodbyes.

Goodbye monarch, swallowtail, and bees.
Hello white grubs beneath the soil, tiny whales
like the curled bodies of Orca in seas
seen one summer before the gusty gales
of their great diminishing. Too much loss
for a decade of century to bear.
The gardener sees, feels and knows the cost.
And yet her green thumb does its healing, shared
amongst the spider lilies and bergamot,
where hummingbirds return from year to year
to this their sanctuary. Were it not
for gardeners on their knees in greening prayer,
only scientists would speak of earth's demise,
but to the gardener, it comes as no surprise.

Spell For A Summer's Night

When Mercury retrogrades at twilight
   buzzing backwards in its orbital dance
      and the Summer Solstice salsas sideways
   while a strawberry moon plumps up in the east,
pick the little berries from the garden you have tended.

Eat them one by one, savoring the magic
   of every living nugget created for your pleasure,
      of every living fruit filled with sun and nourishment
   for you. For you under the stars, for you amidst fireflies,
for you, when the fragrance of last lilacs lingers.

Perhaps you'll hear the whippoorwill's lone call
   or feel the shadow of the night hawk's swooping.
      Perhaps you will recall the lovers of your past, the ones
   who blessed you with the gift of longing or the wisdom
to know what was not meant to be. Yet the spell they cast

informs the heart, like the muse you can't refuse.
   Be grateful for the suffering of love, for without it,
      no bittersweet music, no gypsy jazz, no solo saxophone
   would moan in the secret place beneath your bones.
Eat your bittersweet berries. Be glad in the mad magic
   of a summer's night.

Draw pentacles in the grass and grab a stick for a wand. Wait
   for shooting stars and the demented old fox who no longer
frightens you. Bid him adieu, bless him on his staggered path
   for his days are surely numbered. Remember
all the creatures hidden in trees and dens and grass,
   for they too are the meek inheritors of the night.

At Ding Darling Preserve, Sanibel Island

A reddish heron nestled in the trees—
the first surprise of the sanctuary.
Then plovers, storks, anhinga and ospreys
ride the breeze to land in green waters' estuary.
Protected here, spoon bills sleep on branches.
Great white pelicans plummet, crash their beaks
to catch whatever tasty fish chances
too close to water's edge. Snowy egret
breaks the silence. She dips her fine white bill.
Straight down, straight up, fish slide down curvy throats.
In the lake, a white ibis takes its fill
of luscious fish that fly near fishing boats.
An osprey and an eagle touch the sky
then vanish above the boat—a sleek goodbye.

Sonnet For Summer Surprise

Surprise is a clown with a secret, brings
twists, delays, pockets filled with nickels,
pockets filled with coal, pockets filled with rings
that may or may not fit. Perhaps a pickle
or a jam to nibble or bite into. Surprise
brings something more than expected: a thought,
a song, more time to read, whistle at fire-flies,
give rise to answers long after sought.
Surprise is a bouquet with weeds thrown in:
day lilies, goat's rue, toad flax, wood sorrel.
Surprise is a chartreuse thread, antique pin
that brings good luck. Perhaps the blessed thistle
whose prickles ward off thieves you didn't know
peeped in. Wild molecule. The mutant GO.

O Summer, how I hate to see you go.
Cicadas, crickets shake their tambourines.
Houdini fireflies, hummingbird show.
Indigo twilight, shadow on green beans.
Gold finch pick seeds from prairie cone flowers.
Wild turkeys, wobbly chicks a-trundle.
Azure skies sparkling. Night's greening showers.
Lavender stalks drying in a bundle.
O Summer, do you really have to end?
Goodbye to golden skin and endless day.
Hello to autumn lurking 'round the bend.
Farewell swimming in the sun, glorious play.
Your memory in winter brings us cheer.
It's good to know you resurrect each year.

The Garden Hour

It's enough that Norway maples sway
wind-sizzled though long branches. Enough too
that violets, primrose, and creamy peony
stretch, and trumpet vines blare their deep rue.
It's enough that the rain, April-cool,
pellets the good roof—mazurka of steam
and squirrel's feet. Ivy-lined gutters, drain pipes spool,
splash, slither down the driveway's crooked seam.
Perhaps wisdom grows unexpected as wild grapes
and paradise is a garden returned to bruised.
Yet cardinals flash their tango capes
and maples bud maroon and chartreuse.
Take hold of one more root. Breathe in fragrant flower.
Let worries cease. Embrace this garden hour.

The hummingbird hovers
over ruby bergamot—
soft summer dusks.

Each day another swallowtail
floats by, landing on pink
cone flowers and milk pods.

At the suet, a downy woodpecker
hangs upside-down,
the chickadee rightside-up.

Cottage bound cats curl near
clumps of French lavender and
prairie grasses grown round as hay stacks.

Sparrows land on phlox.
Families of goldfinch pull out
sunflowers from feeders daily.

Butter-and-eggs bloom on wispy stalks,
and every day for no apparent reason—
sun on lilies and black-eyed Susans.

Indigo sky at twilight—
Venus ablaze, and always
the moon in her many corsets.

Days At The Japanese Garden: Haiku Sequence

so many walks here—
invitation to be still
sanctuary calls

pagoda dogwood
with white flowers unfurling—
petal in the wind

along the dark pond
Siberian irises
shooting from jagged rocks

after the April rain
mallard cozied on smooth stone
waiting for the sun

catching the May rain—
feel the waterfall tumbling
hear its happy roar

sun shafts through the clouds
after June evening's drizzle—look!
a rainbow surrounds us

July afternoon
Thai Chi in the pavilion—
forgive me...too hot

ah, it's you again
a little moss behind your ears—
August Buddha at the gate

small bridge over the creek
tea house in September shadows—
listen...it calls to you

chill rippling the pond
soon the winter swans return—
how do they keep warm?

after first snow melt
every shade of green returns—
textured harmony

Still Life

Dawn brings seven doves to scavenge left-over seeds
on the ground below the feeder this gray winter day,
a day that begins like a black and white photo.
Then the coffee and table cream,
the greeting of the cat who wants her dollop,
nearly still in the shadowy kitchen this hazy winter day,
except for the cat's tongue lapping her treat,
our happy morning ritual.
I pray, and imagine the day before us,
stillness settling like a light comforter,
even on this bleak winter day,
here in a crime-filled city in a bankrupt state,
and now a leader
who has been compared to the Joker and Hitler.
How to keep from getting swept beyond reason
in an age too full of misinformation and panic?
How to ward off despair and wait for some good news
or at least a hopeful gesture?
How to lower my standards of civility
to keep claim on the stillness
I have worked so hard to find and for so long?
The cat's detachment wired into her DNA lifts her above it all,
blesses her with an easy escape.
I watch her get on with her simple life.
Later she will curl up next to me and we will be still,
the only sound a little purr
above my shouting heart
in a room where stillness doesn't come easily
on a day where I dread the news,
each announcement a double-edged sword.
And yet, here we are. Still life.

September Slips

September slips its golden tips on trees
that lightly shimmer in September's breeze.
The hummingbirds begin their southern flight,
tiny wings fluttering with all their might.
Orchards yield abundant fruit: honey crisp
as the night grows close and cool, and frost rips
through the pumpkins, grown brightest orange and round.
Milk pod fluff floats and lands on hardened ground,
where soon the sunset maple's leaves will fall.
September is a transitory call,
a golden bridge from season unto season.
If we find ourselves beyond our reason
in someplace in between, we remember
all creatures dance to change in September.

Nygren Carriage Ride

Come ride with me in a horse-drawn carriage
on a country lane in the wild prairie,
past milkweed, bergamot, and prairie sage
wet from afternoon rain. Horses carry
us on our enchanted journey, their hooves
a kind of music make, quaint and merry.
They whinny in slow pace on quiet grooves.
Soft scent of prairie flowers mingle here
where time has lost its intruding touch, where
pelicans may rise up from the river
and, lucky, you might glance a foe and deer
who use the oak's canopy for their rooves.
Soon the sun will set, ablaze in milk clouds.
Soon comes the Milky Way behind the shrouds.

When the fortune teller scowled
at your broken lifeline, you laughed
in that shanty where wood incandesced
like red wands. The old Appalachian,
wrinkled, bald, and bristled, whispered:
Be careful. To me: *I see you at a desk.*

That night a gust blew our tent over
a cliff in the Smokies. You were amused.
I was terrified. You stayed cool
as a willow while my hands quivered
like aspens. As black leaves swirled
and roared, we huddled in the old Pontiac

and wrote notes on Kleenex:
You who have known the storm,
what secret are you howling?
Moonbeam
The secret is in the eye of the storm,
and you are it.
Starlock

We never made it to Mardis Gras.

Forty years later, little monks in orange
grow like great pumpkins in your spirit patch,
not far from my carrots, quilled pens,
pointed inward.

IV-WILD FRUITION

Lately Writing Sonnets

I write imperfect sonnets, like my life,
its lyrical limitations unfold,
an antidote against the varied strife
that winds though joy, longing to be told.
After sixty years of living free verse,
a quiet sense of order now prevails.
Perhaps I am a little bit perverse,
contrarian, or worse. When life derails,
a sonnet is in order. Its borders,
like a budget, live within frugal means.
It builds its house with brick and mortar,
somewhat formally furnished but serene.
Compact, composed and with a quiet voice,
a sonnet sings within its cherished choice.

Sonnet For Live Words

Give me consonants snapping like snare drums,
the difference between a T and a D.
Serve me a whole slice of bread, not just crumbs.
A tangerine's not a dromedary.
Speak vowels tunnel-shaped or sharp as skate blades.
Send me sentences that flow from the top
of the mountain, then roar over cascades.
Let them shout, clear and frothy 'til they stop
for commas: rocks and pebbles that protect
the stream from gushing. Please say what you mean.
Words like water can become polluted
too. Think of language, a gift crisp and clean.
Long for great live words to reel in like fish.
Fry them up, digest them, and be nourished.

At Lake Crescent, Washington

Suppose you find yourself in some in-between space,
where no doors are clearly marked:
Enter here, you who would move forward.
Suppose even the currents of your body lost their way,
and strange manifestations disturbed the waters of your blood,
disrupted the electric currents of your heart,
beating faster than a tom-tom in a wild warrior dance.
The chaos of your pulse and loadstones of fatigue
confuse you in contrapuntal castigations.
Then you might seek a lonely, ravaged place
where two mountains meet at Lake Crescent,
a narrow passageway between them.
Let yourself be ferried on shimmering glacial water
through a narrow portal no matter where it leads.
Know that when you pass through *in-between*
you finally find *serene.*

Walking The Labyrinth At Grace Cathedral

Mystical protection. O, Celtic hearts.
In seven circles of heaven, the planets
orbit in divine order. Round edges
border us on our pilgrimages.
Seekers of the deeper spiral, we listen
as we walk. What guidance, what lesson
lies within the knot? The still, small voice says,
"Life is a wonderful symphony. Say yes
to it." That's it? Now all is music.
Celestial chords and contrapuntal magic.
Grace notes glitter like iridescent wings.
City doves flutter over fountains. The wind sings.
Curled within the labyrinth is a covenant
we keep: a rainbow promise, a song incarnate.

Entering The Chant

I woke this morning from a dream of chanting
   and for a few blessed seconds, bliss enshrouded me
like the protective cocoon of a giant swallowtail.

In the dream I saw the chant – straight dark lines
   like a series of dashes. I heard the chant sung,
a clear, steady bell of voices in unison.

I entered the chant, walking through a white door.
   I wanted to stay in that sacred state,
where my entire life had finally led. Yet

I was not disappointed when I awoke enclosed
   in a blue blanket, a pillow folded beneath
my head, and the day still before me.

Consider

In the fulfillment of joy consider:
the fireflies enchanting the twilight,
monarchs landing softer than a whisper,
as golden rays of the full moon ignite
sleepers' dreams. Night breeze blowing through windows
where dreamers turn softly to each other
in the peaceful sleep on downy pillows.
In the fulfillment of joy, consider:
midnight rain, cardinals' capes, and morning dew,
the lily in fulfillment opening,
the sunflowers exploding too,
stretching always to the sun's beckoning.
Let summer sustain abundance indeed,
fruition of joy in every seed.

Because the price of wisdom is too high—
like trumpet vines in wild fruition,
wisdom tangles and spirals toward the sky
and cannot be controlled. Come, completion
of roots, bulbs, and seeds. Flowers and trees
become, deep within the soil grow.
Essence of red rose in summer's breeze.
Yet inward, wisdom to the rich river
goes, nourished by the inland sea's fresh flow.
Then the receiver becomes the giver.
The price of wisdom is so high because
Paradise is a garden returned to
bruised, where only mercy and nature's laws
inform the heart. Red rose renew.

The Joy Of Unimportance

Let us praise the joy of unimportance,
the gentle sway of leisure, like lilacs
bending in the May breeze. Let's take a chance—
let the day lie before us on its back,
cozy and inviting as a hammock
strung between two big trees with canopies
or a quilted blanket, a picnic, and Bach.
Why not? We're a couple of jalopies
in our sixth decade with no need to rush.
Like wild geraniums, we unfold
in mornings, click ice cubes at evening's hush.
Ah, everything's important when you're old:
Sun, rain, birds, ferns, clogged drain, mail—all equal.
We no longer have to please all people!

Come To The Council Ring
--at the Clearing, in Door County, WI

Come with me to the Council Ring.
We'll sit and talk and then we'll sing
and watch the sun drop coral and pink,
brilliant gold Jacob's ladder link by link
lapping its bronze lullaby on Green Bay.
Here earth, wind, and fire say:
O sit awhile at the Council Ring.
Let go of all the cares you bring
and let the elements heal you now.

Then may the purple dusk take its bow,
nestle you in its crimson rose glow.
As twilight stars alight in indigo,
the steel blue shimmer of bay and Milky Way
are yours for keeps. So sashay
to deep blue sleep, silent as the red fox
along the bluff, still as black inky docks
in gray mist. Then bid good night
to Council Ring and shooting stars. Sleep tight.

The Sweet Spot

Some day you may find yourself
in the sweet spot.
It will not be perfect
but it will be enough.
You and your lover will still snore
but make the best of it,
creating jokes just past midnight,
like "Where's the aardvark?"
or "I hear the rolling thunder,"
but you will still be in the sweet spot,
where, as another poet once said,
there is nothing to dread,
at least not every single day
compared to *before,*
when big time stress, maybe even crisis,
was your daily companion,
the one that power-walked
never strolled through life,
not to mention smelling the lavender
or talking to hummingbirds.

Remember that guy?
The one who woke you from sleep
chattering and chasing you
through murky dreams?
When you're in the sweet spot,
he's gone. Kaput.
It may feel like loss.
You must trust that loss,
redefine it.
Call it emptiness,
the kind the Buddhists seek,
when you are not filled to the brim
with busyness and toil.

Now you have a wide space to enjoy
the fruits of your labor,
the pomegranate to savor,
seed by seed,
big blackberries for breakfast,
and all that wide, wonderful time
on your fingertips. Go ahead.
Enjoy it. Whoever said life
was all about work and toil,
ambition and *more,*
never knew the sweet life--
the long, luxurious meander,
mid-afternoon for no good reason
whatsoever.

Dear Masseuse

You have turned
my toes to velvet mushrooms,
my arches to cotton,
the balls of my feet to Indian drums,
my heels to onyx,
my ankles to pigeon feet,
my calves to oranges,
the back of my knees to creeks,
my thighs to bread dough,
my lumbar to stars,
my spine to piano keys,
my shoulder blades to foothills,
my shoulders to satin ribbon,
the crimp of my neck to root,
my neck to stem,
my head to dandelion,
my hair to fluff,
scattered in the eucalyptus wind.

This Thanksgiving, Remember

Remember the air that made the clouds that made the rain
that watered the ground and made the potatoes
both white and sweet at your Thanksgiving table.

Remember the birds that gave the eggs that gave the meat
that baked in the oven and smelled divine
surrounded by sage dressing at your Thanksgiving table.

Remember the sun that fed the vines that made the wine
that went into long-stemmed glasses and shimmered
near the candles at your Thanksgiving table.

Remember the miners who culled the silver and the fire
that molded the precious metal that became a spoon
so perfectly set around your Thanksgiving table.

Remember the migrants who picked the lemons that you slice
in water with ice, and who carried the pumpkins that whipped
into the pie at your Thanksgiving table.

Remember the cows for all their kindnesses: the cream,
the milk, the cheese, and the chocolate that finished
the meal at your Thanksgiving table. Dare not forget:

All pilgrims who seek the higher life in strange
and wonderful places. All the invisible faces
of those gone on, the homeless, and the struggling,

our blue planet, that most special place in the universe,
where we the lucky thrive amidst rivers and orchards
where fruit hangs in perfect abundant globes.

I Want The Time

I want the time to slow things down,
meander through a Wisconsin town,
dilly dally the morning away,
read romances on a rainy day.

I want the time to make new friends,
lollygag around, run errands:
farmers' markets, hardware stores,
libraries, antique shops galore.

I want the time to write a book,
perhaps a letter to Amy Zook,
bake a chocolate cake from scratch,
make sure that my pillows match.

I want the time to pamper pets,
do what I love with no regrets,
pen a poem, steep some tea,
take the time to trim a tree.

I want the time to clean my home,
finally tackle that enormous tome,
spend some time with a manatee,
try my hand at calligraphy.

I want the time to tend the garden:
tulips, lilies, slice of heaven.
Hanging baskets on the patio,
Patsy Kline on the radio.

I want the time to decorate
and let my skin exfoliate.
Grapevine garlands, wreaths hand wound,
yarrow, rosebud, hound's tooth round.

I want the time to think about
the people I can't do without.
I want to give them more of me
and know the best is yet to be.

Summer Solstice

A pair of Green Angel Wing butterflies cavort around the pear tree. Everywhere another shade of green pipes a Celtic jig. A patch of catnip lures a tawny Angora cat with a gorgeous black mask. I love to see him roll in the driveway, chase the crows who have eaten the spring-pink, bristly strawberries. Raccoons resume nightly marauding, lead their kin to the skylight to peep down on us. Now the air's obese with birdsong and peonies, and day-sleeping fireflies cradled on leaves. I sleep in too, listen to obscure female singers whose names escape me. Plans slip away, disappear like barrel slugs. Sunset brings angel wings. Mars travels closer to the earth, blinks by Antares, now bright as a field lily. A Question Mark Angel Wing butterfly cozies on my arm. Listen. Nighthawks whistle. The squirrels change from red to gray. Listen. The earth says yes and no and yes again.

Secret Shaman

Better to be a secret shaman
who looks meek but whose soul
is as tall as a redwood and as old
than a dilettante who samples
but doesn't find
the still consistency within.

You don't need to travel
half way around the world
to meet the guru of your dreams
when the secret shaman within
already whispers your name.

Better to be a secret shaman
searching the inconsistencies
and lazy hypocrisies
passed off as enlightenment
to those who might be impressed.

You don't need to switch
from tribe to tribe
to find the secret language
you are longing for.
Each day the earth sends you
friends and grace
among the trees and fields.

The Benevolence

Believe in the benevolence of bees
and bergamot beckoning hummingbirds.
Hail the tiny ones who sail thousands
of treacherous miles to return to us each year.
Rely on the wisdom of crows who congregate
on catalpa trees for their alarms are righteous.
Shout amen to each alleluia tree and branches
bearing fruit, turning leaves, holding nests.
Give thanks to the rain and the sun that dance
in contrapuntal perfection their never ending fugue.
Bless each lady bug and firefly for without them
summer would hold less magic in the Midwest.
Glory be to the swallowtail and monarch
and every short but mysterious life.
All gratitude to the gardeners great and small,
the cultivators and creators, here and above.
Let us never forget the wind, great breath of life.
O, what benevolence bestowed on us each day,
given to us without expectation of pay.

Grateful acknowledgement is made to the editors of the journals in which these poems first appeared or were republished:

AMERICAN MASSAGE JOURNAL: *Dear Masseuse*

THE AVOCET: *February Morning, The Long Winter Procrastinates, Snow Salsa, Hummingbird Whisperer, O Summer, Consider, Winter's Favor, Great River Road*

CASA DE CINCA HERMANAS: *Blue-Jinxed 1, A Few Ways of Looking at Rage, Santa Fe Logic, Convertible Mind on the High Road to Taos*

CHIRON REVIEW: *Ask the Gardener* (Pushcart nomination), *Cosmic Stew Diptych, A Few Ways of Looking at Deception, What Sedona Says* (Pushcart nomination), *Spell for a Summer's Night* (Pushcart nomination), *One October Past Your Prime*

BACK TO JOY (a June Cotner Book): *Embrace Uncertainty, At Lake Crescent*

EARTH BLESSINGS (a June Cotner Book): *Hummingbird Whisperer*

ENGLISH JOURNAL: *Sonnet for Live Words*

GARDEN BLESSINGS (a June Cotner Book): *The Garden Hour*

GRATITIUDE PRAYERS (a June Cotner Book): *At the Sacred Cliffs of Kauai*

JANE'S STORIES IV: *Bridges*

LITTLE EAGLE VERSE: *The Long Winter Procrastinates, Cheating Grief*

MARKET STREET PRESS: *Why She Can't Sleep, Texting Terrorist*

MINOTAUR: *Snow Salsa, September Slips, The Joy of Unimportance, The Sweet Spot, Dangerous Woman*

NATIONAL LAND INSTITUTE NEWSLETTER: *Nygren Prairie Carriage Ride*

NEW YORK TIMES COMMENTARY, Donald Trump Poetry Contest: *Still Life*

OUT OF LINE: *This Thanksgiving, Remember*

PUDDING MAGAZINE: *Begin with the Faucet*

PENINSULA PULSE: *At Three Arch Cape* (Hal Grutzmacher Poetry Award)

ROCK RIVER TIMES: *January Spell, February Morning, Winter's Favor, O Summer, Wild Fruition, About Time, Unwinding the Old Year*

SEDONA BIZ: *What Sedona Says*

SPOON RIVER QUARTERLY: *Before Grooming the Horse in Winter*

SOUNDINGS: *Paradigm Shift in the Pacific Northwest*

TAMBOURINE: *The Butterfly Tree*

WIND: *Point of Departure*

WORD OF ART: *Hummingbird Whisperer* (honorable mention), *September Slips*

The following pieces also appeared in:

THE ALLELUIA TREE (collection) from Puddin'head Press: *Embrace Uncertainty, Paradigm Shift in the Pacific Northwest, At the Sacred Cliffs of Kauai, Cheating Grief, Bridges, Entering the Chant*

WHO WALKS AMONG THE TREES WITH CHARITY (collection) from Wind Publications: *The Butterfly Tree*

TONIGHT ON THIS LATE ROAD from Erie Street Press: *Backroads*

INVISIBLE STRING from Erie Street Press: *Moonbeam and Starlock.*

Christine Swanberg has published several books of poetry: *Tonight on This Late Road*, (Erie Street, 1984). *Invisible String* (Erie Street, 1990), *Bread Upon the Waters* (UW:Whitewater, 1990), *Slow Miracle* (Lake Shore, 1992), *The Tenderness of Memory* (Plainview Press, 1995), *The Red Lacquer Room* (Chiron Press, 2001), and *Who Walks Among the Trees with Charity* (Wind Publications, 2005), and *The Alleluia Tree* from Puddin'head Press, 2012. Hundreds of her poems appear in anthologies such as *Knowing Stones: Poems of Exotic Travel; I am Becoming the Woman I've Wanted: Jane's Stories; Key West: an Anthology;* and *Still Going Strong* and journals such as *Lilipoh, Spoon River Quarterly, Beloit Poetry Journal, Casa de Cinco Hermanas, The Avocet, Chiron, Kansas Quarterly, Creative Woman, Earth's Daughters, Sow's Ear, Wind* and many others.

She received the Rockford Area Arts Council Lawrence Gloyd Award for Community Impact. Earlier awards include the YWCA Award for the Arts and the Womanspace Womanspirit Award. She has received numerous grants through the Rockford Area Arts Council. Poet's Market featured a full-length interview with her. She has contributed chapters to *Women on Poetry* and *Writing After Retirement.* After winning the Poetswest invitation to read at the Frye Museum in 2000, she has been a regular poetry presenter in various venues in the Pacific Northwest as well as WSER radio there. She has received numerous awards for her poetry throughout the years.

A writing teacher in public schools, colleges, museums, and *The Clearing,* and mentor for forty years, Christine's students have been successful. Christine has had residencies at Centrum Center for the Arts in Port Townsend, WA. She has recently given readings in Sedona AZ, which featured a full-length article in *Kudos Magazine;* Taos NM, and many bookstores, libraries, and community organizations throughout the country as well as NPR/WNIU.

Christine's publications, readings, radio presentations, editorial experience, collaborations, and other public presentations cast a wide net. She is public poet with the ability to create poems that are both accessible and lyrical. Her writing is meant to be a shared rather than strictly personal adventure.

She loves gardening, day trips, singing with community choruses, swimming, walking on the beach, vintage restoration and traveling with her husband of 45 years, Jeffrey, whose photos appear in this collection and on the cover.